Zoom™ In on
Dogs

Labrador Retrievers

Leo Statts

abdopublishing.com

Published by Abdo Zoom™, PO Box 398166, Minneapolis, Minnesota 55439. Copyright © 2017 by Abdo Consulting Group, Inc. International copyrights reserved in all countries. No part of this book may be reproduced in any form without written permission from the publisher. Abdo Zoom™ is a trademark and logo of Abdo Consulting Group, Inc.

Printed in the United States of America, North Mankato, Minnesota
062016
092016

THIS BOOK CONTAINS RECYCLED MATERIALS

Cover Photo: Olga Ovcharenko/Shutterstock Images
Interior Photos: Shutterstock Images, 1, 4, 9, 10, 11, 12, 16–17, 19; Jaromir Chalabala/Shutterstock Images, 5; C. Byatt-Norman/Shutterstock Images, 6–7; Waldemar Dabrowski/Shutterstock Images, 8; Wong Yu Liang/Shutterstock Images, 13; Marcella Miriello/Shutterstock Images, 15; Red Line Editorial, 20 (left), 20 (right), 21 (left), 21 (right)

Editor: Brienna Rossiter
Series Designer: Madeline Berger
Art Direction: Dorothy Toth

Publisher's Cataloging-in-Publication Data
Names: Statts, Leo, author.
Title: Labrador retrievers / by Leo Statts.
Description: Minneapolis, MN : Abdo Zoom, [2017] | Series: Dogs | Includes
    bibliographical references and index.
Identifiers: LCCN 2016941145 | ISBN 9781680791754 (lib. bdg.) |
    ISBN 9781680793437 (ebook) | ISBN 9781680794328 (Read-to-me ebook)|Subjects: LCSH: Labrador
retrievers--Juvenile literature.
Classification: DDC 636.752--dc23
LC record available at http://lccn.loc.gov/2016941145

Table of Contents

Labrador Retrievers

Labrador retrievers are a popular dog breed.

They are also called labs. Labs are friendly and loyal. They are also loving.

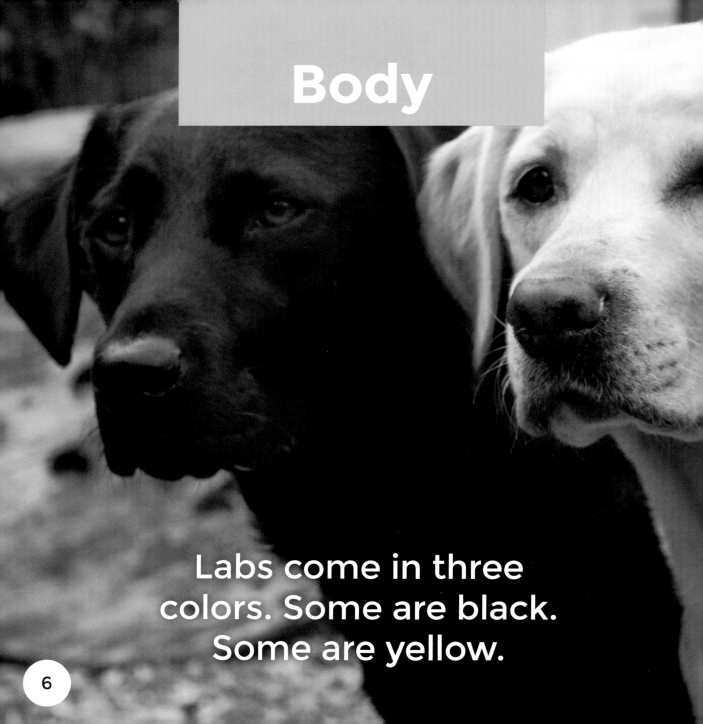

Body

Labs come in three colors. Some are black. Some are yellow.

Others are brown.
Their fur looks like the
color of chocolate.

Labs are big dogs.

They can weigh
100 pounds (45 kg).

Care

Labs are very active.

They need exercise
every day. They like to
run and swim.

Their fur sheds a lot.

They should be brushed once a week.

Personality

Labs are smart. They can
be **trained** to do jobs.
Some are guide dogs.

Others are
rescue dogs.

They like to hold objects in their mouths. But they are gentle.

History

Labrador is an area in Canada. But labs came from Newfoundland. That is also in Canada.

Labs were **bred** to be
hunting dogs.

Quick Stats

Average Weight

A Labrador retriever weighs more than a full suitcase.

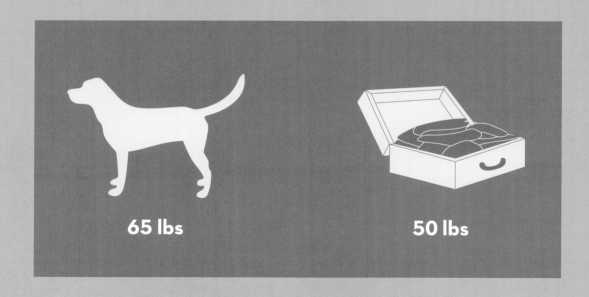

65 lbs

50 lbs

Average Height

A Labrador retriever is shorter than an acoustic guitar.

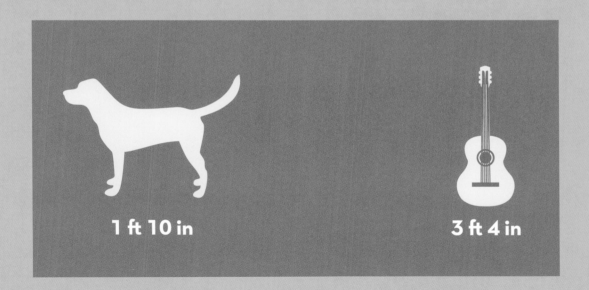

1 ft 10 in

3 ft 4 in

Glossary

active - busy or energetic.

bred - raised so that it will have a special kind of look or feature.

breed - a group of animals sharing the same looks and features.

gentle - calm and sweet.

loyal - faithful to a person or idea.

shed - when hair or skin falls off an animal's body.

trained - taught to do something.

Booklinks

For more information on Labrador retrievers, please visit booklinks.abdopublishing.com

 In on Animals!

Learn even more with the Abdo Zoom Animals database. Check out abdozoom.com for more information.

Index